GREETINGS FROM NORTH DAKOTA
AN ADDRESS AND DATE BOOK
From the postcard collections of Lawrence Aasen and Ronald Olin.

Copyright © 2006
North Dakota Institute for Regional Studies
http://www.lib.ndsu.nodak.edu/ndirs/

178.—Girls' Dormitory State Normal School, Mayville, N. D.

MAYVILLE

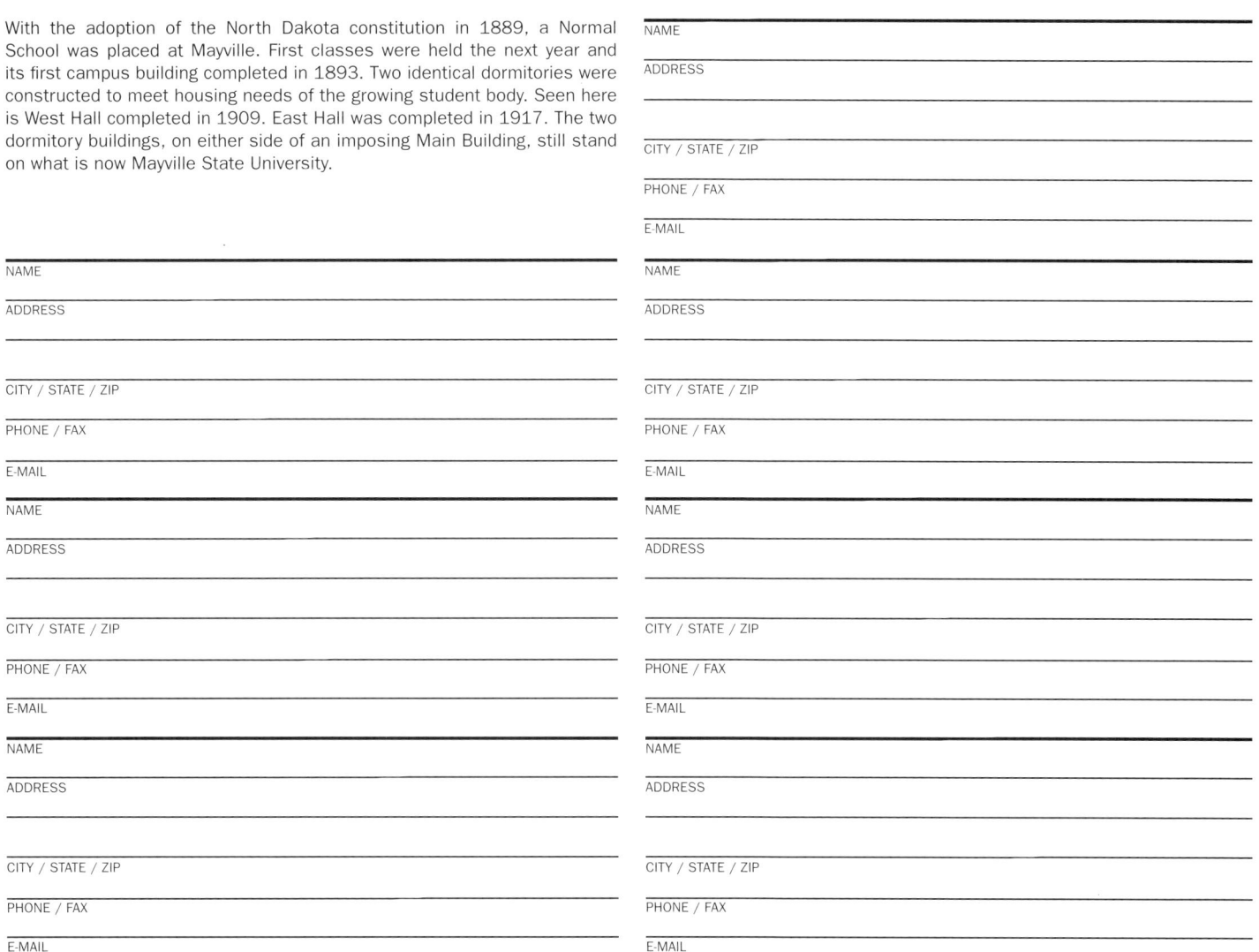

With the adoption of the North Dakota constitution in 1889, a Normal School was placed at Mayville. First classes were held the next year and its first campus building completed in 1893. Two identical dormitories were constructed to meet housing needs of the growing student body. Seen here is West Hall completed in 1909. East Hall was completed in 1917. The two dormitory buildings, on either side of an imposing Main Building, still stand on what is now Mayville State University.

A

NAME

ADDRESS

CITY / STATE / ZIP

PHONE / FAX

E-MAIL

NAME

ADDRESS

CITY / STATE / ZIP

PHONE / FAX

E-MAIL

NAME

ADDRESS

CITY / STATE / ZIP

PHONE / FAX

E-MAIL

NAME

ADDRESS

CITY / STATE / ZIP

PHONE / FAX

E-MAIL

NAME

ADDRESS

CITY / STATE / ZIP

PHONE / FAX

E-MAIL

NAME

ADDRESS

CITY / STATE / ZIP

PHONE / FAX

E-MAIL

NAME

ADDRESS

CITY / STATE / ZIP

PHONE / FAX

E-MAIL

A

NAME

ADDRESS

CITY / STATE / ZIP

PHONE / FAX

E-MAIL

NAME

ADDRESS

CITY / STATE / ZIP

PHONE / FAX

E-MAIL

NAME

ADDRESS

CITY / STATE / ZIP

PHONE / FAX

E-MAIL

NAME

ADDRESS

CITY / STATE / ZIP

PHONE / FAX

E-MAIL

NAME

ADDRESS

CITY / STATE / ZIP

PHONE / FAX

E-MAIL

NAME

ADDRESS

CITY / STATE / ZIP

PHONE / FAX

E-MAIL

NAME

ADDRESS

CITY / STATE / ZIP

PHONE / FAX

E-MAIL

NAME

ADDRESS

CITY / STATE / ZIP

PHONE / FAX

E-MAIL

A

NAME	NAME
ADDRESS	ADDRESS
CITY / STATE / ZIP	CITY / STATE / ZIP
PHONE / FAX	PHONE / FAX
E-MAIL	E-MAIL
NAME	NAME
ADDRESS	ADDRESS
CITY / STATE / ZIP	CITY / STATE / ZIP
PHONE / FAX	PHONE / FAX
E-MAIL	E-MAIL
NAME	NAME
ADDRESS	ADDRESS
CITY / STATE / ZIP	CITY / STATE / ZIP
PHONE / FAX	PHONE / FAX
E-MAIL	E-MAIL
NAME	NAME
ADDRESS	ADDRESS
CITY / STATE / ZIP	CITY / STATE / ZIP
PHONE / FAX	PHONE / FAX
E-MAIL	E-MAIL

A

NAME

ADDRESS

CITY / STATE / ZIP

PHONE / FAX

E-MAIL

Public education began at Hillsboro in 1881 with 59 students attending an ungraded school. Soon there was a call for a high school, and in 1891, high school courses were offered. A new public school was completed and 300 students were enrolled in November 1893. Hancock Brothers, Fargo, designed the school. They were proud of the design and used it in their advertising. A wing was added in 1916 to accommodate student population growth. The school continued to serve the educational needs of the Hillsboro community until a new school was built in 1966.

NAME

ADDRESS

CITY / STATE / ZIP

PHONE / FAX

E-MAIL

NAME

ADDRESS

CITY / STATE / ZIP

PHONE / FAX

E-MAIL

NAME

ADDRESS

CITY / STATE / ZIP

PHONE / FAX

E-MAIL

NAME

ADDRESS

CITY / STATE / ZIP

PHONE / FAX

E-MAIL

NAME

ADDRESS

CITY / STATE / ZIP

PHONE / FAX

E-MAIL

NAME

ADDRESS

CITY / STATE / ZIP

PHONE / FAX

E-MAIL

HIGH SCHOOL, HILLSBORO, N.D.

HILLSBORO

113.—Old Lee Mill on the Sheyenne, Aneta, N. D.

ANETA

The Lee Mill and dam were erected on the Sheyenne River in 1884, a short distance south of where it crosses the Nelson-Griggs county line. The mill was owned and operated first by Nels C. Rukke. Rukke thought the community urgently needed a mill, since there wasn't a facility within 40 miles that could grind feed and flour for the growing number of homesteaders. The Lee Mill no longer exists; however, there still are stones at the site where the building once stood.

B

NAME

ADDRESS

CITY / STATE / ZIP

PHONE / FAX

E-MAIL

NAME

ADDRESS

CITY / STATE / ZIP

PHONE / FAX

E-MAIL

NAME

ADDRESS

CITY / STATE / ZIP

PHONE / FAX

E-MAIL

NAME

ADDRESS

CITY / STATE / ZIP

PHONE / FAX

E-MAIL

NAME

ADDRESS

CITY / STATE / ZIP

PHONE / FAX

E-MAIL

NAME

ADDRESS

CITY / STATE / ZIP

PHONE / FAX

E-MAIL

NAME

ADDRESS

CITY / STATE / ZIP

PHONE / FAX

E-MAIL

B

NAME

ADDRESS

CITY / STATE / ZIP

PHONE / FAX

E-MAIL

NAME

ADDRESS

CITY / STATE / ZIP

PHONE / FAX

E-MAIL

NAME

ADDRESS

CITY / STATE / ZIP

PHONE / FAX

E-MAIL

NAME

ADDRESS

CITY / STATE / ZIP

PHONE / FAX

E-MAIL

NAME

ADDRESS

CITY / STATE / ZIP

PHONE / FAX

E-MAIL

NAME

ADDRESS

CITY / STATE / ZIP

PHONE / FAX

E-MAIL

NAME

ADDRESS

CITY / STATE / ZIP

PHONE / FAX

E-MAIL

NAME

ADDRESS

CITY / STATE / ZIP

PHONE / FAX

E-MAIL

B

NAME

ADDRESS

CITY / STATE / ZIP

PHONE / FAX

E-MAIL

NAME

ADDRESS

CITY / STATE / ZIP

PHONE / FAX

E-MAIL

NAME

ADDRESS

CITY / STATE / ZIP

PHONE / FAX

E-MAIL

NAME

ADDRESS

CITY / STATE / ZIP

PHONE / FAX

E-MAIL

NAME

ADDRESS

CITY / STATE / ZIP

PHONE / FAX

E-MAIL

NAME

ADDRESS

CITY / STATE / ZIP

PHONE / FAX

E-MAIL

NAME

ADDRESS

CITY / STATE / ZIP

PHONE / FAX

E-MAIL

NAME

ADDRESS

CITY / STATE / ZIP

PHONE / FAX

E-MAIL

B

The Western Bohemian Fraternal Association, Herman Lodge, No. 30, was organized in Lidgerwood in 1897. It was the first of its order in North Dakota. As the membership increased, it became necessary to construct a permanent lodge building. The Bohemian Hall was constructed in 1908, a place where people of Czech heritage could gather, speak their language and celebrate special events. The building also was used for high school commencements, basketball games and plays. As the demographics changed, interest in the club faded and its membership dropped. The club sold the lodge building in 1974, with all future meetings at the Lidgerwood Civic Center.

NAME

ADDRESS

CITY / STATE / ZIP

PHONE / FAX

E-MAIL

NAME

ADDRESS

CITY / STATE / ZIP

PHONE / FAX

E-MAIL

NAME

ADDRESS

CITY / STATE / ZIP

PHONE / FAX

E-MAIL

NAME

ADDRESS

CITY / STATE / ZIP

PHONE / FAX

E-MAIL

NAME

ADDRESS

CITY / STATE / ZIP

PHONE / FAX

E-MAIL

NAME

ADDRESS

CITY / STATE / ZIP

PHONE / FAX

E-MAIL

NAME

ADDRESS

CITY / STATE / ZIP

PHONE / FAX

E-MAIL

Bohemian Hall, Lidgerwood, N. D.

LIDGERWOOD

Part of Christine, N. D.

CHRISTINE

Norwegian and Swedish settlers founded the village of Christine in 1883 on the Milwaukee Road Railroad line. The town is located on a parcel of land between the Red River of the North and the Wild Rice River and has never been incorporated. It is uncertain as to who "Christine" was. Some folks claimed it was named for Christine Nilsson, a Swedish opera singer. Others claimed it was for Kristine Norby, wife of an early pioneer. This view from around 1915 was taken from the Christine Lutheran Church steeple.

C

NAME

ADDRESS

CITY / STATE / ZIP

PHONE / FAX

E-MAIL

NAME

ADDRESS

CITY / STATE / ZIP

PHONE / FAX

E-MAIL

NAME

ADDRESS

CITY / STATE / ZIP

PHONE / FAX

E-MAIL

NAME

ADDRESS

CITY / STATE / ZIP

PHONE / FAX

E-MAIL

NAME

ADDRESS

CITY / STATE / ZIP

PHONE / FAX

E-MAIL

NAME

ADDRESS

CITY / STATE / ZIP

PHONE / FAX

E-MAIL

NAME

ADDRESS

CITY / STATE / ZIP

PHONE / FAX

E-MAIL

C

NAME	NAME
ADDRESS	ADDRESS
CITY / STATE / ZIP	CITY / STATE / ZIP
PHONE / FAX	PHONE / FAX
E-MAIL	E-MAIL
NAME	NAME
ADDRESS	ADDRESS
CITY / STATE / ZIP	CITY / STATE / ZIP
PHONE / FAX	PHONE / FAX
E-MAIL	E-MAIL
NAME	NAME
ADDRESS	ADDRESS
CITY / STATE / ZIP	CITY / STATE / ZIP
PHONE / FAX	PHONE / FAX
E-MAIL	E-MAIL
NAME	NAME
ADDRESS	ADDRESS
CITY / STATE / ZIP	CITY / STATE / ZIP
PHONE / FAX	PHONE / FAX
E-MAIL	E-MAIL

C

NAME	NAME
ADDRESS	ADDRESS
CITY / STATE / ZIP	CITY / STATE / ZIP
PHONE / FAX	PHONE / FAX
E-MAIL	E-MAIL

NAME	NAME
ADDRESS	ADDRESS
CITY / STATE / ZIP	CITY / STATE / ZIP
PHONE / FAX	PHONE / FAX
E-MAIL	E-MAIL

NAME	NAME
ADDRESS	ADDRESS
CITY / STATE / ZIP	CITY / STATE / ZIP
PHONE / FAX	PHONE / FAX
E-MAIL	E-MAIL

NAME	NAME
ADDRESS	ADDRESS
CITY / STATE / ZIP	CITY / STATE / ZIP
PHONE / FAX	PHONE / FAX
E-MAIL	E-MAIL

C

The community of Flasher probably would not exist if it had not been for William H. Brown who organized the Brown Land Company in 1901 to encourage the settlement of southwestern North Dakota. He focused on bringing families to the area from the North Central United States using the slogan, "Out They Go to North Dakota." Brown plotted the town site of Flasher in 1902, naming it after Mable Flasher Vrooman, his niece and secretary.

2114 Flasher, N. Dak.

FLASHER

SWIMMING POOL, RIVERSIDE PARK, MINOT, N. D.

104361

MINOT

This view of the swimming pool at Riverside Park was taken about 1922. Riverside Park, located on the Mouse River, is the largest of Minot's city parks. The property that comprises the park was purchased by the city in 1912. It not only contained a swimming pool, but also a zoo and an automobile drive following the river. After the death of Theodore Roosevelt, the park district changed the name to Roosevelt Park in September 1922. Sculptor J. Phimister Proctor was commissioned to create a statue of Roosevelt that was placed in the park on a pedestal designed to represent the geological formations of the Badlands.

D

NAME

ADDRESS

CITY / STATE / ZIP

PHONE / FAX

E-MAIL

NAME

ADDRESS

CITY / STATE / ZIP

PHONE / FAX

E-MAIL

NAME

ADDRESS

CITY / STATE / ZIP

PHONE / FAX

E-MAIL

NAME

ADDRESS

CITY / STATE / ZIP

PHONE / FAX

E-MAIL

NAME

ADDRESS

CITY / STATE / ZIP

PHONE / FAX

E-MAIL

NAME

ADDRESS

CITY / STATE / ZIP

PHONE / FAX

E-MAIL

NAME

ADDRESS

CITY / STATE / ZIP

PHONE / FAX

E-MAIL

D

NAME

ADDRESS

CITY / STATE / ZIP

PHONE / FAX

E-MAIL

NAME

ADDRESS

CITY / STATE / ZIP

PHONE / FAX

E-MAIL

NAME

ADDRESS

CITY / STATE / ZIP

PHONE / FAX

E-MAIL

NAME

ADDRESS

CITY / STATE / ZIP

PHONE / FAX

E-MAIL

NAME

ADDRESS

CITY / STATE / ZIP

PHONE / FAX

E-MAIL

NAME

ADDRESS

CITY / STATE / ZIP

PHONE / FAX

E-MAIL

NAME

ADDRESS

CITY / STATE / ZIP

PHONE / FAX

E-MAIL

NAME

ADDRESS

CITY / STATE / ZIP

PHONE / FAX

E-MAIL

D

NAME

ADDRESS

CITY / STATE / ZIP

PHONE / FAX

E-MAIL

NAME

ADDRESS

CITY / STATE / ZIP

PHONE / FAX

E-MAIL

NAME

ADDRESS

CITY / STATE / ZIP

PHONE / FAX

E-MAIL

NAME

ADDRESS

CITY / STATE / ZIP

PHONE / FAX

E-MAIL

NAME

ADDRESS

CITY / STATE / ZIP

PHONE / FAX

E-MAIL

NAME

ADDRESS

CITY / STATE / ZIP

PHONE / FAX

E-MAIL

NAME

ADDRESS

CITY / STATE / ZIP

PHONE / FAX

E-MAIL

NAME

ADDRESS

CITY / STATE / ZIP

PHONE / FAX

E-MAIL

D

The Great Northern Railroad platted Rugby Junction in July 1886. It was named for Rugby, Warwickshire, England. The town's most famous claim to fame is that it is located in the geographical center of North America. This fact was established in January 1931 by the U.S. Department of Interior, and published in Geological Survey Bulletin 817. A pyramid-shaped field stone cairn marks the site and is a popular tourist stop. This postcard taken around 1910 shows Rugby's busy railroad district with its grain elevators and depot.

NAME

ADDRESS

CITY / STATE / ZIP

PHONE / FAX

E-MAIL

NAME

ADDRESS

CITY / STATE / ZIP

PHONE / FAX

E-MAIL

NAME

ADDRESS

CITY / STATE / ZIP

PHONE / FAX

E-MAIL

NAME

ADDRESS

CITY / STATE / ZIP

PHONE / FAX

E-MAIL

NAME

ADDRESS

CITY / STATE / ZIP

PHONE / FAX

E-MAIL

NAME

ADDRESS

CITY / STATE / ZIP

PHONE / FAX

E-MAIL

NAME

ADDRESS

CITY / STATE / ZIP

PHONE / FAX

E-MAIL

Bird's Eye View of Rugby, N. Dak. from top of the Schoolhouse looking North-East

RUGBY

High School, Edgeley, N. D.

EDGELEY

The first school building in Edgeley was a frame two-story, two-room structure. A more substantial brick school was built in summer 1905. The old school house was moved to a new location and served as the Edgeley town hall, American Legion and the Public Library. The school district went under the name Golden Glen School District until 1959 when it reorganized and brought in students from a large area in both La Moure and Dickey counties.

E
F

NAME

ADDRESS

CITY / STATE / ZIP

PHONE / FAX

E-MAIL

NAME

ADDRESS

CITY / STATE / ZIP

PHONE / FAX

E-MAIL

NAME

ADDRESS

CITY / STATE / ZIP

PHONE / FAX

E-MAIL

NAME

ADDRESS

CITY / STATE / ZIP

PHONE / FAX

E-MAIL

NAME

ADDRESS

CITY / STATE / ZIP

PHONE / FAX

E-MAIL

NAME

ADDRESS

CITY / STATE / ZIP

PHONE / FAX

E-MAIL

NAME

ADDRESS

CITY / STATE / ZIP

PHONE / FAX

E-MAIL

E
F

NAME	NAME
ADDRESS	ADDRESS
CITY / STATE / ZIP	CITY / STATE / ZIP
PHONE / FAX	PHONE / FAX
E-MAIL	E-MAIL
NAME	NAME
ADDRESS	ADDRESS
CITY / STATE / ZIP	CITY / STATE / ZIP
PHONE / FAX	PHONE / FAX
E-MAIL	E-MAIL
NAME	NAME
ADDRESS	ADDRESS
CITY / STATE / ZIP	CITY / STATE / ZIP
PHONE / FAX	PHONE / FAX
E-MAIL	E-MAIL
NAME	NAME
ADDRESS	ADDRESS
CITY / STATE / ZIP	CITY / STATE / ZIP
PHONE / FAX	PHONE / FAX
E-MAIL	E-MAIL

E F

NAME		NAME	
ADDRESS		ADDRESS	
CITY / STATE / ZIP		CITY / STATE / ZIP	
PHONE / FAX		PHONE / FAX	
E-MAIL		E-MAIL	
NAME		NAME	
ADDRESS		ADDRESS	
CITY / STATE / ZIP		CITY / STATE / ZIP	
PHONE / FAX		PHONE / FAX	
E-MAIL		E-MAIL	
NAME		NAME	
ADDRESS		ADDRESS	
CITY / STATE / ZIP		CITY / STATE / ZIP	
PHONE / FAX		PHONE / FAX	
E-MAIL		E-MAIL	
NAME		NAME	
ADDRESS		ADDRESS	
CITY / STATE / ZIP		CITY / STATE / ZIP	
PHONE / FAX		PHONE / FAX	
E-MAIL		E-MAIL	

E
F

Cattle ranching is closely linked with the development of southwestern North Dakota. Visitors traveling through the region on the newly constructed Northern Pacific Railway realized its potential as cattle country. Easterners provided investment money and by the 1880s millions of cattle were grazing the North Dakota Badlands. Cattle drives from states to the south also came north to take advantage of plentiful grass, streams and natural protection afforded by numerous ravines and coulees. Theodore Roosevelt who established and operated a ranch there between 1883 and 1886, was the best-known cattle rancher in the region.

NAME
ADDRESS
CITY / STATE / ZIP
PHONE / FAX
E-MAIL

NAME
ADDRESS
CITY / STATE / ZIP
PHONE / FAX
E-MAIL

NAME
ADDRESS
CITY / STATE / ZIP
PHONE / FAX
E-MAIL

NAME
ADDRESS
CITY / STATE / ZIP
PHONE / FAX
E-MAIL

NAME
ADDRESS
CITY / STATE / ZIP
PHONE / FAX
E-MAIL

NAME
ADDRESS
CITY / STATE / ZIP
PHONE / FAX
E-MAIL

NAME
ADDRESS
CITY / STATE / ZIP
PHONE / FAX
E-MAIL

Cattle Range near Dickinson, No. Dak.

DICKINSON

"Public School & Dietz Residence, New Salem, N. D."
"Pub. for Wiegman Mercantile Co., New Salem, N. D." — Printed in Germany

NEW SALEM

New Salem was settled in 1883 by an Evangelical church group from Germany, organized by a church colonization bureau in Chicago. School classes began in 1884 with instruction initially in German. Classes later were held in English three days a week and in German two days a week. The Hancock Brothers of Fargo designed a new building that was completed in 1903. It served the educational needs of the community until 1965 when a new high school was built. The unique style of the Albert Dietz home reflects one of the town's prominent business leaders. He and his family emigrated directly from Germany to New Salem in the early 1890s and established a lumber, grain and farm machinery business.

G

NAME

ADDRESS

CITY / STATE / ZIP

PHONE / FAX

E-MAIL

NAME

ADDRESS

CITY / STATE / ZIP

PHONE / FAX

E-MAIL

NAME

ADDRESS

CITY / STATE / ZIP

PHONE / FAX

E-MAIL

NAME

ADDRESS

CITY / STATE / ZIP

PHONE / FAX

E-MAIL

NAME

ADDRESS

CITY / STATE / ZIP

PHONE / FAX

E-MAIL

NAME

ADDRESS

CITY / STATE / ZIP

PHONE / FAX

E-MAIL

NAME

ADDRESS

CITY / STATE / ZIP

PHONE / FAX

E-MAIL

G

NAME

ADDRESS

CITY / STATE / ZIP

PHONE / FAX

E-MAIL

Henry C. Koch of Milwaukee, Wis., designed this Gothic-Revival structure. It was built in 1883 and used by Dakota Territory legislators as they prepared for statehood. There was some hope at the time that Jamestown would become North Dakota's capitol city, but this was not to be. The structure served as the Stutsman County Courthouse for nearly 100 years. A new facility was built in 1982. The building was saved from the wrecking ball. It is the oldest surviving courthouse in the state and is listed on the National Register of Historic Places.

NAME	NAME
ADDRESS	ADDRESS
CITY / STATE / ZIP	CITY / STATE / ZIP
PHONE / FAX	PHONE / FAX
E-MAIL	E-MAIL
NAME	NAME
ADDRESS	ADDRESS
CITY / STATE / ZIP	CITY / STATE / ZIP
PHONE / FAX	PHONE / FAX
E-MAIL	E-MAIL
NAME	NAME
ADDRESS	ADDRESS
CITY / STATE / ZIP	CITY / STATE / ZIP
PHONE / FAX	PHONE / FAX
E-MAIL	E-MAIL

Court House and Jail, Jamestown, N. Dak.

JAMESTOWN

BERTHOLD

The Great Northern Railroad established a station along the tracks about 25 miles west of Minot in April 1900. A post office was established in October that same year, and the village was incorporated in 1902. Berthold was named for Fort Berthold, which was named for a trading post operator, Bartholomew Berthold. This photomontage, postmarked in 1915, shows some of Berthold's important community buildings at that time.

H

NAME

ADDRESS

CITY / STATE / ZIP

PHONE / FAX

E-MAIL

NAME

ADDRESS

CITY / STATE / ZIP

PHONE / FAX

E-MAIL

NAME

ADDRESS

CITY / STATE / ZIP

PHONE / FAX

E-MAIL

NAME

ADDRESS

CITY / STATE / ZIP

PHONE / FAX

E-MAIL

NAME

ADDRESS

CITY / STATE / ZIP

PHONE / FAX

E-MAIL

NAME

ADDRESS

CITY / STATE / ZIP

PHONE / FAX

E-MAIL

NAME

ADDRESS

CITY / STATE / ZIP

PHONE / FAX

E-MAIL

H

NAME

ADDRESS

CITY / STATE / ZIP

PHONE / FAX

E-MAIL

NAME

ADDRESS

CITY / STATE / ZIP

PHONE / FAX

E-MAIL

NAME

ADDRESS

CITY / STATE / ZIP

PHONE / FAX

E-MAIL

NAME

ADDRESS

CITY / STATE / ZIP

PHONE / FAX

E-MAIL

NAME

ADDRESS

CITY / STATE / ZIP

PHONE / FAX

E-MAIL

NAME

ADDRESS

CITY / STATE / ZIP

PHONE / FAX

E-MAIL

NAME

ADDRESS

CITY / STATE / ZIP

PHONE / FAX

E-MAIL

NAME

ADDRESS

CITY / STATE / ZIP

PHONE / FAX

E-MAIL

H

NAME

ADDRESS

CITY / STATE / ZIP

PHONE / FAX

E-MAIL

NAME

ADDRESS

CITY / STATE / ZIP

PHONE / FAX

E-MAIL

NAME

ADDRESS

CITY / STATE / ZIP

PHONE / FAX

E-MAIL

NAME

ADDRESS

CITY / STATE / ZIP

PHONE / FAX

E-MAIL

NAME

ADDRESS

CITY / STATE / ZIP

PHONE / FAX

E-MAIL

NAME

ADDRESS

CITY / STATE / ZIP

PHONE / FAX

E-MAIL

NAME

ADDRESS

CITY / STATE / ZIP

PHONE / FAX

E-MAIL

NAME

ADDRESS

CITY / STATE / ZIP

PHONE / FAX

E-MAIL

H

As the Great Northern Railroad was being built through the area in 1896, enterprising settlers developed two town sites, Gilbert and Walker, a short distance from one another along the proposed railroad line. Because there already was a town named Walker on the railroad line, it was changed to Finley in honor of J.B. Finley, a railroad company official. Owners of the Finley town site bought out Gilbert in January 1897, and the villages were combined under the name of Finley. This view is of Main Street taken around 1910.

NAME

ADDRESS

CITY / STATE / ZIP

PHONE / FAX

E-MAIL

NAME

ADDRESS

CITY / STATE / ZIP

PHONE / FAX

E-MAIL

NAME

ADDRESS

CITY / STATE / ZIP

PHONE / FAX

E-MAIL

NAME

ADDRESS

CITY / STATE / ZIP

PHONE / FAX

E-MAIL

NAME

ADDRESS

CITY / STATE / ZIP

PHONE / FAX

E-MAIL

NAME

ADDRESS

CITY / STATE / ZIP

PHONE / FAX

E-MAIL

NAME

ADDRESS

CITY / STATE / ZIP

PHONE / FAX

E-MAIL

Main Street, Finley, N. Dak.

FINLEY

HATTON

The first settlers arrived in the Hatton area in 1874, homesteading along the banks of the Goose River. The community quickly became a center for Norwegian Americans seeking the rich farm lands of the Red River Valley. Hatton was established in 1884 with the arrival of the Great Northern Railroad. Seen here are the business district, churches and homes, including the childhood home of famed Arctic aviator, Carl Ben Eielson, which is now a museum.

I

J

NAME

ADDRESS

CITY / STATE / ZIP

PHONE / FAX

E-MAIL

NAME

ADDRESS

CITY / STATE / ZIP

PHONE / FAX

E-MAIL

NAME

ADDRESS

CITY / STATE / ZIP

PHONE / FAX

E-MAIL

NAME

ADDRESS

CITY / STATE / ZIP

PHONE / FAX

E-MAIL

NAME

ADDRESS

CITY / STATE / ZIP

PHONE / FAX

E-MAIL

NAME

ADDRESS

CITY / STATE / ZIP

PHONE / FAX

E-MAIL

I
J

NAME	NAME
ADDRESS	ADDRESS
CITY / STATE / ZIP	CITY / STATE / ZIP
PHONE / FAX	PHONE / FAX
E-MAIL	E-MAIL
NAME	NAME
ADDRESS	ADDRESS
CITY / STATE / ZIP	CITY / STATE / ZIP
PHONE / FAX	PHONE / FAX
E-MAIL	E-MAIL
NAME	NAME
ADDRESS	ADDRESS
CITY / STATE / ZIP	CITY / STATE / ZIP
PHONE / FAX	PHONE / FAX
E-MAIL	E-MAIL
NAME	NAME
ADDRESS	ADDRESS
CITY / STATE / ZIP	CITY / STATE / ZIP
PHONE / FAX	PHONE / FAX
E-MAIL	E-MAIL

I
J

NAME	NAME
ADDRESS	ADDRESS
CITY / STATE / ZIP	CITY / STATE / ZIP
PHONE / FAX	PHONE / FAX
E-MAIL	E-MAIL
NAME	NAME
ADDRESS	ADDRESS
CITY / STATE / ZIP	CITY / STATE / ZIP
PHONE / FAX	PHONE / FAX
E-MAIL	E-MAIL
NAME	NAME
ADDRESS	ADDRESS
CITY / STATE / ZIP	CITY / STATE / ZIP
PHONE / FAX	PHONE / FAX
E-MAIL	E-MAIL
NAME	NAME
ADDRESS	ADDRESS
CITY / STATE / ZIP	CITY / STATE / ZIP
PHONE / FAX	PHONE / FAX
E-MAIL	E-MAIL

I
J

NAME

ADDRESS

CITY / STATE / ZIP

PHONE / FAX

E-MAIL

The Northern Pacific Railroad crossed the Red River into Dakota Territory in 1872 and established the town of Fargo. A new railroad depot designed by well-known architect Cass Gilbert was built in 1897. Parks were developed on both sides of the depot, no doubt to give railroad travelers a positive first-impression of the town. Directly across the street from the depot are two of Fargo's "skyscrapers," the deLendrecie's department store with the corner cupola and the Waldorf Hotel, the finest hotel in Fargo at the time of this view, circa 1910.

NAME

ADDRESS

CITY / STATE / ZIP

PHONE / FAX

E-MAIL

NAME

ADDRESS

CITY / STATE / ZIP

PHONE / FAX

E-MAIL

NAME

ADDRESS

CITY / STATE / ZIP

PHONE / FAX

E-MAIL

NAME

ADDRESS

CITY / STATE / ZIP

PHONE / FAX

E-MAIL

NAME

ADDRESS

CITY / STATE / ZIP

PHONE / FAX

E-MAIL

NAME

ADDRESS

CITY / STATE / ZIP

PHONE / FAX

E-MAIL

N. P. Depot Park and Skyscrapers, Fargo, N. Dak.

FARGO

Public School, Walhalla, N.D.

WALHALLA

Walhalla is located in the scenic Pembina River Valley near the Canadian border. Its name comes from Valhalla, home of the Norse gods. Its beginnings go back to 1845 when Father Belcourt built a log church and school at the site. At that time it was called St. Joseph and also was a major point on the Red River oxcart trails between Canada and St. Paul, Minn. Twin schools, one an elementary school and the other a high school, were built side-by-side in about 1910 for the growing student population. The first high school graduating class was in 1911 with one student graduating. The school was replaced in 1936 with a two-story brick structure.

K

NAME

ADDRESS

CITY / STATE / ZIP

PHONE / FAX

E-MAIL

NAME

ADDRESS

CITY / STATE / ZIP

PHONE / FAX

E-MAIL

NAME

ADDRESS

CITY / STATE / ZIP

PHONE / FAX

E-MAIL

NAME

ADDRESS

CITY / STATE / ZIP

PHONE / FAX

E-MAIL

NAME

ADDRESS

CITY / STATE / ZIP

PHONE / FAX

E-MAIL

NAME

ADDRESS

CITY / STATE / ZIP

PHONE / FAX

E-MAIL

NAME

ADDRESS

CITY / STATE / ZIP

PHONE / FAX

E-MAIL

K

NAME	NAME
ADDRESS	ADDRESS
CITY / STATE / ZIP	CITY / STATE / ZIP
PHONE / FAX	PHONE / FAX
E-MAIL	E-MAIL

NAME	NAME
ADDRESS	ADDRESS
CITY / STATE / ZIP	CITY / STATE / ZIP
PHONE / FAX	PHONE / FAX
E-MAIL	E-MAIL

NAME	NAME
ADDRESS	ADDRESS
CITY / STATE / ZIP	CITY / STATE / ZIP
PHONE / FAX	PHONE / FAX
E-MAIL	E-MAIL

NAME	NAME
ADDRESS	ADDRESS
CITY / STATE / ZIP	CITY / STATE / ZIP
PHONE / FAX	PHONE / FAX
E-MAIL	E-MAIL

K

NAME	NAME
ADDRESS	ADDRESS
CITY / STATE / ZIP	CITY / STATE / ZIP
PHONE / FAX	PHONE / FAX
E-MAIL	E-MAIL
NAME	NAME
ADDRESS	ADDRESS
CITY / STATE / ZIP	CITY / STATE / ZIP
PHONE / FAX	PHONE / FAX
E-MAIL	E-MAIL
NAME	NAME
ADDRESS	ADDRESS
CITY / STATE / ZIP	CITY / STATE / ZIP
PHONE / FAX	PHONE / FAX
E-MAIL	E-MAIL
NAME	NAME
ADDRESS	ADDRESS
CITY / STATE / ZIP	CITY / STATE / ZIP
PHONE / FAX	PHONE / FAX
E-MAIL	E-MAIL

K

NAME

ADDRESS

CITY / STATE / ZIP

PHONE / FAX

E-MAIL

Dann P. Barnes came to Glen Ullin in 1883 when the town consisted of only one frame building and several tents. Barnes saw there was a need for lumber to build the fledgling town. He went to Minneapolis and purchased three carloads of lumber and started the Barnes Lumber Co. The entrepreneur formed a partnership with John T. Nelson in 1890 and opened the Barnes & Nelson General Store, that supplied the community with almost anything a person would need. This postcard shows the brick structure used by the business from 1905 to 1917.

NAME

ADDRESS

CITY / STATE / ZIP

PHONE / FAX

E-MAIL

NAME

ADDRESS

CITY / STATE / ZIP

PHONE / FAX

E-MAIL

NAME

ADDRESS

CITY / STATE / ZIP

PHONE / FAX

E-MAIL

NAME

ADDRESS

CITY / STATE / ZIP

PHONE / FAX

E-MAIL

NAME

ADDRESS

CITY / STATE / ZIP

PHONE / FAX

E-MAIL

NAME

ADDRESS

CITY / STATE / ZIP

PHONE / FAX

E-MAIL

Barnes & Nelson Block, Glenullin, N. D.

GLEN ULLIN

View of N. P. Depot from top of Northwest Hotel, Bismarck, N. D. — 1908

BISMARCK

The Northern Pacific Railroad arrived in Bismarck on the Missouri River June 5, 1873. Train cars were transported across the river on ferryboats until a bridge was completed over the Missouri in 1882. Tracks were laid over the frozen river ice during winter. The railroad depot was completed in 1901 in the Spanish architectural style. Located along Main Avenue, it was situated in the heart of the Bismarck business district. Railroad passenger service stopped in 1979 when Amtrak eliminated the North Coast Limited.

L

NAME

ADDRESS

CITY / STATE / ZIP

PHONE / FAX

E-MAIL

NAME

ADDRESS

CITY / STATE / ZIP

PHONE / FAX

E-MAIL

NAME

ADDRESS

CITY / STATE / ZIP

PHONE / FAX

E-MAIL

NAME

ADDRESS

CITY / STATE / ZIP

PHONE / FAX

E-MAIL

NAME

ADDRESS

CITY / STATE / ZIP

PHONE / FAX

E-MAIL

NAME

ADDRESS

CITY / STATE / ZIP

PHONE / FAX

E-MAIL

NAME

ADDRESS

CITY / STATE / ZIP

PHONE / FAX

E-MAIL

L

NAME

ADDRESS

CITY / STATE / ZIP

PHONE / FAX

E-MAIL

NAME

ADDRESS

CITY / STATE / ZIP

PHONE / FAX

E-MAIL

NAME

ADDRESS

CITY / STATE / ZIP

PHONE / FAX

E-MAIL

NAME

ADDRESS

CITY / STATE / ZIP

PHONE / FAX

E-MAIL

NAME

ADDRESS

CITY / STATE / ZIP

PHONE / FAX

E-MAIL

NAME

ADDRESS

CITY / STATE / ZIP

PHONE / FAX

E-MAIL

NAME

ADDRESS

CITY / STATE / ZIP

PHONE / FAX

E-MAIL

NAME

ADDRESS

CITY / STATE / ZIP

PHONE / FAX

E-MAIL

L

NAME	NAME
ADDRESS	ADDRESS
CITY / STATE / ZIP	CITY / STATE / ZIP
PHONE / FAX	PHONE / FAX
E-MAIL	E-MAIL
NAME	NAME
ADDRESS	ADDRESS
CITY / STATE / ZIP	CITY / STATE / ZIP
PHONE / FAX	PHONE / FAX
E-MAIL	E-MAIL
NAME	NAME
ADDRESS	ADDRESS
CITY / STATE / ZIP	CITY / STATE / ZIP
PHONE / FAX	PHONE / FAX
E-MAIL	E-MAIL
NAME	NAME
ADDRESS	ADDRESS
CITY / STATE / ZIP	CITY / STATE / ZIP
PHONE / FAX	PHONE / FAX
E-MAIL	E-MAIL

L

The town of McKinney was established in 1883. Located on the Souris (Mouse) River, it became an important stopping point for most of the early settlers in the area. The dam and adjacent park were popular gathering points in the early 1900s. Fourth of July celebrations held at this site were outstanding events, with every homesteader coming from miles around. Presidential candidate Eugene Debs came to speak at the 1903 celebration. One such event was captured in this 1904 postcard. Note the boat merry-go-round operated by water power from the dam. The post office closed in 1916 and the town died. All remaining buildings were torn down in 1935 when the valley was purchased for a wildlife refuge.

NAME

ADDRESS

CITY / STATE / ZIP

PHONE / FAX

E-MAIL

NAME

ADDRESS

CITY / STATE / ZIP

PHONE / FAX

E-MAIL

NAME

ADDRESS

CITY / STATE / ZIP

PHONE / FAX

E-MAIL

NAME

ADDRESS

CITY / STATE / ZIP

PHONE / FAX

E-MAIL

NAME

ADDRESS

CITY / STATE / ZIP

PHONE / FAX

E-MAIL

NAME

ADDRESS

CITY / STATE / ZIP

PHONE / FAX

E-MAIL

NAME

ADDRESS

CITY / STATE / ZIP

PHONE / FAX

E-MAIL

Mouse River and Dam at Mc. Kinney N. D.

McKINNEY

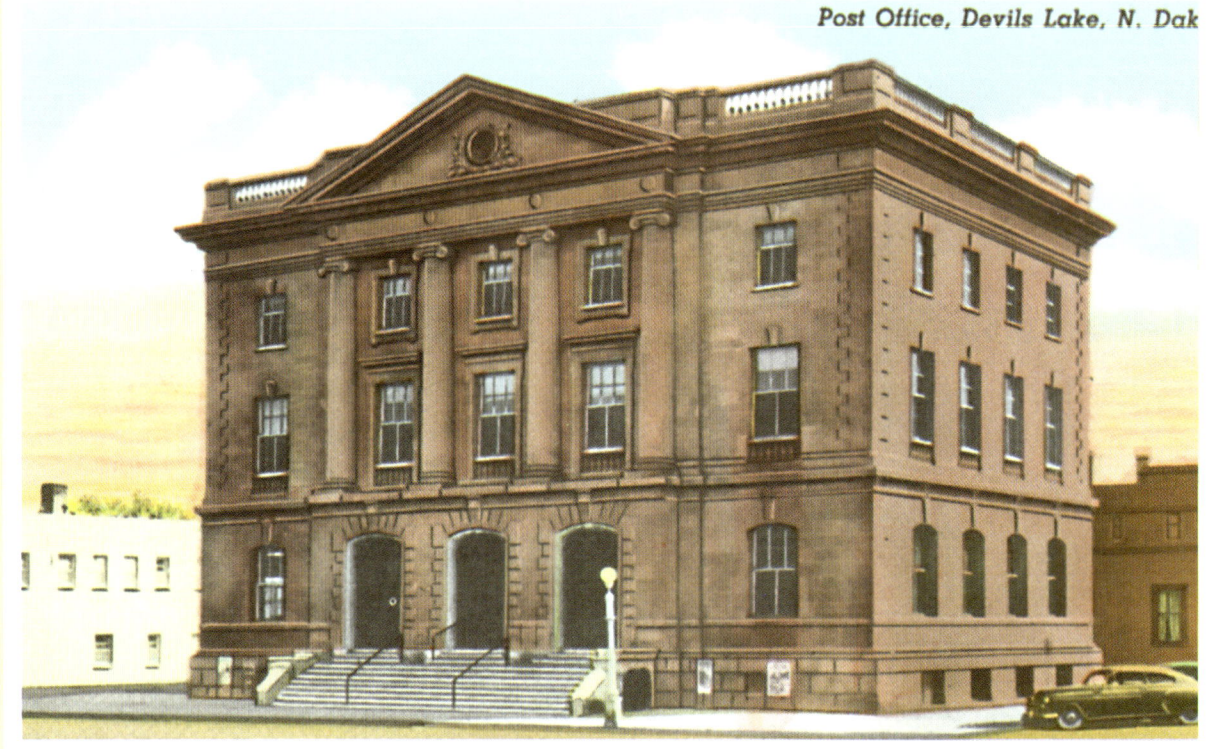

Post Office, Devils Lake, N. Dak

DEVILS LAKE

The U.S. Post Office and Courthouse is a cultural and artistic landmark in the Devils Lake community and region. Local resident U.S. Sen. H.C. Hansbrough secured federal funding, construction began in 1908, and it opened for use in April 1910. Built in the Greek Revival style of Vermont limestone, the lobby featured a vaulted ceiling. The building served as the post office for the community until November 1977 when a new facility was built. Realizing its historic significance, it was purchased by the Lake Region Heritage Center in 1977 and houses historical exhibits and an art gallery. The building was placed on the National Register of Historic Places in 1978.

M

NAME

ADDRESS

CITY / STATE / ZIP

PHONE / FAX

E-MAIL

NAME

ADDRESS

CITY / STATE / ZIP

PHONE / FAX

E-MAIL

NAME

ADDRESS

CITY / STATE / ZIP

PHONE / FAX

E-MAIL

NAME

ADDRESS

CITY / STATE / ZIP

PHONE / FAX

E-MAIL

NAME

ADDRESS

CITY / STATE / ZIP

PHONE / FAX

E-MAIL

NAME

ADDRESS

CITY / STATE / ZIP

PHONE / FAX

E-MAIL

NAME

ADDRESS

CITY / STATE / ZIP

PHONE / FAX

E-MAIL

M

NAME
ADDRESS
CITY / STATE / ZIP
PHONE / FAX
E-MAIL

NAME
ADDRESS
CITY / STATE / ZIP
PHONE / FAX
E-MAIL

NAME
ADDRESS
CITY / STATE / ZIP
PHONE / FAX
E-MAIL

NAME
ADDRESS
CITY / STATE / ZIP
PHONE / FAX
E-MAIL

NAME
ADDRESS
CITY / STATE / ZIP
PHONE / FAX
E-MAIL

NAME
ADDRESS
CITY / STATE / ZIP
PHONE / FAX
E-MAIL

NAME
ADDRESS
CITY / STATE / ZIP
PHONE / FAX
E-MAIL

NAME
ADDRESS
CITY / STATE / ZIP
PHONE / FAX
E-MAIL

NAME	NAME	**M**
ADDRESS	ADDRESS	
CITY / STATE / ZIP	CITY / STATE / ZIP	
PHONE / FAX	PHONE / FAX	
E-MAIL	E-MAIL	
NAME	NAME	
ADDRESS	ADDRESS	
CITY / STATE / ZIP	CITY / STATE / ZIP	
PHONE / FAX	PHONE / FAX	
E-MAIL	E-MAIL	
NAME	NAME	
ADDRESS	ADDRESS	
CITY / STATE / ZIP	CITY / STATE / ZIP	
PHONE / FAX	PHONE / FAX	
E-MAIL	E-MAIL	
NAME	NAME	
ADDRESS	ADDRESS	
CITY / STATE / ZIP	CITY / STATE / ZIP	
PHONE / FAX	PHONE / FAX	
E-MAIL	E-MAIL	

M

The story of Crosby is a tale of two cities. The Crosby town site was platted at the terminus of the Great Northern Railroad in 1903. A few years later the Soo Line Railroad platted a town named Imperial three miles east, the name implying it was the more dominant of the two communities. The village of Crosby moved one mile east in 1908, at the crossing point of the two railroads, an act that would soon absorb Imperial. Crosby became the Divide county seat in 1912, making it the most prominent town in the county.

NAME

ADDRESS

CITY / STATE / ZIP

PHONE / FAX

E-MAIL

NAME

ADDRESS

CITY / STATE / ZIP

PHONE / FAX

E-MAIL

NAME

ADDRESS

CITY / STATE / ZIP

PHONE / FAX

E-MAIL

NAME

ADDRESS

CITY / STATE / ZIP

PHONE / FAX

E-MAIL

NAME

ADDRESS

CITY / STATE / ZIP

PHONE / FAX

E-MAIL

NAME

ADDRESS

CITY / STATE / ZIP

PHONE / FAX

E-MAIL

NAME

ADDRESS

CITY / STATE / ZIP

PHONE / FAX

E-MAIL

East Side Residence Section, Crosby, N. D.

CROSBY

High School - LaMoure, N. D.

LaMoure

The first classes for the children of LaMoure began in 1883 only a year after the town's founding. A wood-frame school was built in 1885, and this brick school, costing $50,000, was built in 1905. It served the community's educational needs more than 60 years until 1969 when it was torn down and replaced by a new school complex.

N

NAME

ADDRESS

CITY / STATE / ZIP

PHONE / FAX

E-MAIL

NAME

ADDRESS

CITY / STATE / ZIP

PHONE / FAX

E-MAIL

NAME

ADDRESS

CITY / STATE / ZIP

PHONE / FAX

E-MAIL

NAME

ADDRESS

CITY / STATE / ZIP

PHONE / FAX

E-MAIL

NAME

ADDRESS

CITY / STATE / ZIP

PHONE / FAX

E-MAIL

NAME

ADDRESS

CITY / STATE / ZIP

PHONE / FAX

E-MAIL

NAME

ADDRESS

CITY / STATE / ZIP

PHONE / FAX

E-MAIL

N

NAME

ADDRESS

CITY / STATE / ZIP

PHONE / FAX

E-MAIL

NAME

ADDRESS

CITY / STATE / ZIP

PHONE / FAX

E-MAIL

NAME

ADDRESS

CITY / STATE / ZIP

PHONE / FAX

E-MAIL

NAME

ADDRESS

CITY / STATE / ZIP

PHONE / FAX

E-MAIL

NAME

ADDRESS

CITY / STATE / ZIP

PHONE / FAX

E-MAIL

NAME

ADDRESS

CITY / STATE / ZIP

PHONE / FAX

E-MAIL

NAME

ADDRESS

CITY / STATE / ZIP

PHONE / FAX

E-MAIL

NAME

ADDRESS

CITY / STATE / ZIP

PHONE / FAX

E-MAIL

N

NAME	NAME
ADDRESS	ADDRESS
CITY / STATE / ZIP	CITY / STATE / ZIP
PHONE / FAX	PHONE / FAX
E-MAIL	E-MAIL
NAME	NAME
ADDRESS	ADDRESS
CITY / STATE / ZIP	CITY / STATE / ZIP
PHONE / FAX	PHONE / FAX
E-MAIL	E-MAIL
NAME	NAME
ADDRESS	ADDRESS
CITY / STATE / ZIP	CITY / STATE / ZIP
PHONE / FAX	PHONE / FAX
E-MAIL	E-MAIL
NAME	NAME
ADDRESS	ADDRESS
CITY / STATE / ZIP	CITY / STATE / ZIP
PHONE / FAX	PHONE / FAX
E-MAIL	E-MAIL

N

Old Main on the North Dakota State College of Science campus was built in 1891 by the Red River Valley University, a Methodist college. Authorized at Wahpeton in the North Dakota Constitution, a "Scientific School," rented space in the west wing in 1903 and purchased it in 1905. The building has been used for numerous purposes throughout the college's history, including library, bookstore, dormitory, classrooms and administration offices. The first trade and technical programs were offered at the school in 1922. This program provided a practical, hands-on education for its students, which has proven desirable to employers throughout the country. The school's name was changed to North Dakota State College of Science in 1987.

NAME

ADDRESS

CITY / STATE / ZIP

PHONE / FAX

E-MAIL

NAME

ADDRESS

CITY / STATE / ZIP

PHONE / FAX

E-MAIL

NAME

ADDRESS

CITY / STATE / ZIP

PHONE / FAX

E-MAIL

NAME

ADDRESS

CITY / STATE / ZIP

PHONE / FAX

E-MAIL

NAME

ADDRESS

CITY / STATE / ZIP

PHONE / FAX

E-MAIL

NAME

ADDRESS

CITY / STATE / ZIP

PHONE / FAX

E-MAIL

NAME

ADDRESS

CITY / STATE / ZIP

PHONE / FAX

E-MAIL

Science School, Wahpeton, N. D.

Published by J. J. Keou, Druggist, Wahpeton, N. D.

WAHPETON

Bird's Eye View of Enderlin, N. D.

ENDERLIN

The town site of Enderlin was founded in 1892. There are several theories on how the city got its name. The most intriguing one is that the town was named "end der line" by German railroad workers because it was the terminus of the branch line. This view of Enderlin was taken about 1905 overlooking Baxter Park from one of Enderlin's grain elevators.

O

NAME

ADDRESS

CITY / STATE / ZIP

PHONE / FAX

E-MAIL

NAME

ADDRESS

CITY / STATE / ZIP

PHONE / FAX

E-MAIL

NAME

ADDRESS

CITY / STATE / ZIP

PHONE / FAX

E-MAIL

NAME

ADDRESS

CITY / STATE / ZIP

PHONE / FAX

E-MAIL

NAME

ADDRESS

CITY / STATE / ZIP

PHONE / FAX

E-MAIL

NAME

ADDRESS

CITY / STATE / ZIP

PHONE / FAX

E-MAIL

NAME

ADDRESS

CITY / STATE / ZIP

PHONE / FAX

E-MAIL

O

NAME

ADDRESS

CITY / STATE / ZIP

PHONE / FAX

E-MAIL

NAME

ADDRESS

CITY / STATE / ZIP

PHONE / FAX

E-MAIL

NAME

ADDRESS

CITY / STATE / ZIP

PHONE / FAX

E-MAIL

NAME

ADDRESS

CITY / STATE / ZIP

PHONE / FAX

E-MAIL

NAME

ADDRESS

CITY / STATE / ZIP

PHONE / FAX

E-MAIL

NAME

ADDRESS

CITY / STATE / ZIP

PHONE / FAX

E-MAIL

NAME

ADDRESS

CITY / STATE / ZIP

PHONE / FAX

E-MAIL

NAME

ADDRESS

CITY / STATE / ZIP

PHONE / FAX

E-MAIL

NAME	NAME
ADDRESS	ADDRESS
CITY / STATE / ZIP	CITY / STATE / ZIP
PHONE / FAX	PHONE / FAX
E-MAIL	E-MAIL
NAME	NAME
ADDRESS	ADDRESS
CITY / STATE / ZIP	CITY / STATE / ZIP
PHONE / FAX	PHONE / FAX
E-MAIL	E-MAIL
NAME	NAME
ADDRESS	ADDRESS
CITY / STATE / ZIP	CITY / STATE / ZIP
PHONE / FAX	PHONE / FAX
E-MAIL	E-MAIL
NAME	NAME
ADDRESS	ADDRESS
CITY / STATE / ZIP	CITY / STATE / ZIP
PHONE / FAX	PHONE / FAX
E-MAIL	E-MAIL

O

O

NAME

ADDRESS

CITY / STATE / ZIP

PHONE / FAX

E-MAIL

The North Dakota Agricultural College, now North Dakota State University, was founded in 1890. It also is the home of the North Dakota Agricultural Experiment Station and the NDSU Extension Service. Students were enrolled not only in agriculture but also engineering, home economics, pharmacy, chemistry and the arts and sciences. This 1936 collage features the most prominent buildings on the campus, all of which are still standing. They surround a view of the campus entrance with wrought-iron gates designed by the campus blacksmith. The gates lead to Old Main, the oldest campus building.

NAME

ADDRESS

CITY / STATE / ZIP

PHONE / FAX

E-MAIL

NAME

ADDRESS

CITY / STATE / ZIP

PHONE / FAX

E-MAIL

NAME

ADDRESS

CITY / STATE / ZIP

PHONE / FAX

E-MAIL

NAME

ADDRESS

CITY / STATE / ZIP

PHONE / FAX

E-MAIL

NAME

ADDRESS

CITY / STATE / ZIP

PHONE / FAX

E-MAIL

NAME

ADDRESS

CITY / STATE / ZIP

PHONE / FAX

E-MAIL

266   SOME OF THE MAIN COLLEGE BUILDINGS, AGRICULTURE COLLEGE, FARGO, N. D.

6A-H1058

FARGO

Kirkwood Hotel, Carrington, No. Dak.

CARRINGTON

The Kirkwood Hotel, owned and operated by Mrs. Catherine Kirkwood McConahey, opened for business Nov. 5, 1883. The large 52-room, three-story building was elegantly furnished and earned a reputation as one of the finest hotels in Dakota Territory. Unfortunately, the first Kirkwood Hotel existed a little more than a month when it was destroyed by fire. A near duplicate of the original structure was built on the same site. It remained a popular hostelry until it also was destroyed by fire March 18, 1920.

P

NAME

ADDRESS

CITY / STATE / ZIP

PHONE / FAX

E-MAIL

NAME

ADDRESS

CITY / STATE / ZIP

PHONE / FAX

E-MAIL

NAME

ADDRESS

CITY / STATE / ZIP

PHONE / FAX

E-MAIL

NAME

ADDRESS

CITY / STATE / ZIP

PHONE / FAX

E-MAIL

NAME

ADDRESS

CITY / STATE / ZIP

PHONE / FAX

E-MAIL

NAME

ADDRESS

CITY / STATE / ZIP

PHONE / FAX

E-MAIL

NAME

ADDRESS

CITY / STATE / ZIP

PHONE / FAX

E-MAIL

P

NAME	NAME
ADDRESS	ADDRESS
CITY / STATE / ZIP	CITY / STATE / ZIP
PHONE / FAX	PHONE / FAX
E-MAIL	E-MAIL
NAME	NAME
ADDRESS	ADDRESS
CITY / STATE / ZIP	CITY / STATE / ZIP
PHONE / FAX	PHONE / FAX
E-MAIL	E-MAIL
NAME	NAME
ADDRESS	ADDRESS
CITY / STATE / ZIP	CITY / STATE / ZIP
PHONE / FAX	PHONE / FAX
E-MAIL	E-MAIL
NAME	NAME
ADDRESS	ADDRESS
CITY / STATE / ZIP	CITY / STATE / ZIP
PHONE / FAX	PHONE / FAX
E-MAIL	E-MAIL

P

NAME	NAME
ADDRESS	ADDRESS
CITY / STATE / ZIP	CITY / STATE / ZIP
PHONE / FAX	PHONE / FAX
E-MAIL	E-MAIL
NAME	NAME
ADDRESS	ADDRESS
CITY / STATE / ZIP	CITY / STATE / ZIP
PHONE / FAX	PHONE / FAX
E-MAIL	E-MAIL
NAME	NAME
ADDRESS	ADDRESS
CITY / STATE / ZIP	CITY / STATE / ZIP
PHONE / FAX	PHONE / FAX
E-MAIL	E-MAIL
NAME	NAME
ADDRESS	ADDRESS
CITY / STATE / ZIP	CITY / STATE / ZIP
PHONE / FAX	PHONE / FAX
E-MAIL	E-MAIL

P

NAME

ADDRESS

CITY / STATE / ZIP

PHONE / FAX

E-MAIL

Winters are cold in North Dakota and coal was the primary heating fuel in its early history, primarily lignite coal from the western part of the state. It was a severe winter in 1907. Heavy snow in early February prevented the train from traveling to Munich, located along the Canadian border in Cavalier County, and residents were running short of coal. When a train did arrive with four cars of coal, the residents learned it was destined for another town farther down the line. With an angry crowd at the station, future U.S. Sen. Usher L. Burdick commandeered one of the cars and distributed the coal to those in need, collecting the money and turning it over to the railroad.

NAME

ADDRESS

CITY / STATE / ZIP

PHONE / FAX

E-MAIL

NAME

ADDRESS

CITY / STATE / ZIP

PHONE / FAX

E-MAIL

NAME

ADDRESS

CITY / STATE / ZIP

PHONE / FAX

E-MAIL

NAME

ADDRESS

CITY / STATE / ZIP

PHONE / FAX

E-MAIL

NAME

ADDRESS

CITY / STATE / ZIP

PHONE / FAX

E-MAIL

NAME

ADDRESS

CITY / STATE / ZIP

PHONE / FAX

E-MAIL

When the Coal-Train Arrived at Munich Feb. 8-'07

1907

MUNICH

Alkabo, Divide County, North Dakota.

ALKABO

Located in the northwest corner of North Dakota, the town of Alkabo was founded along the Soo Line Railroad in 1913. Its name was derived from the combination of two soil types prevalent in the area, Alkali and Gumbo. Although the European American settlement didn't begin in the area until 1905, the nearby Writing Rock petroglyphs attest to an earlier thriving prehistoric Indian culture.

Q
R

NAME

ADDRESS

CITY / STATE / ZIP

PHONE / FAX

E-MAIL

NAME

ADDRESS

CITY / STATE / ZIP

PHONE / FAX

E-MAIL

NAME

ADDRESS

CITY / STATE / ZIP

PHONE / FAX

E-MAIL

NAME

ADDRESS

CITY / STATE / ZIP

PHONE / FAX

E-MAIL

NAME

ADDRESS

CITY / STATE / ZIP

PHONE / FAX

E-MAIL

NAME

ADDRESS

CITY / STATE / ZIP

PHONE / FAX

E-MAIL

NAME

ADDRESS

CITY / STATE / ZIP

PHONE / FAX

E-MAIL

Q R

NAME	NAME
ADDRESS	ADDRESS
CITY / STATE / ZIP	CITY / STATE / ZIP
PHONE / FAX	PHONE / FAX
E-MAIL	E-MAIL
NAME	NAME
ADDRESS	ADDRESS
CITY / STATE / ZIP	CITY / STATE / ZIP
PHONE / FAX	PHONE / FAX
E-MAIL	E-MAIL
NAME	NAME
ADDRESS	ADDRESS
CITY / STATE / ZIP	CITY / STATE / ZIP
PHONE / FAX	PHONE / FAX
E-MAIL	E-MAIL
NAME	NAME
ADDRESS	ADDRESS
CITY / STATE / ZIP	CITY / STATE / ZIP
PHONE / FAX	PHONE / FAX
E-MAIL	E-MAIL

Q R

NAME	NAME
ADDRESS	ADDRESS
CITY / STATE / ZIP	CITY / STATE / ZIP
PHONE / FAX	PHONE / FAX
E-MAIL	E-MAIL
NAME	NAME
ADDRESS	ADDRESS
CITY / STATE / ZIP	CITY / STATE / ZIP
PHONE / FAX	PHONE / FAX
E-MAIL	E-MAIL
NAME	NAME
ADDRESS	ADDRESS
CITY / STATE / ZIP	CITY / STATE / ZIP
PHONE / FAX	PHONE / FAX
E-MAIL	E-MAIL
NAME	NAME
ADDRESS	ADDRESS
CITY / STATE / ZIP	CITY / STATE / ZIP
PHONE / FAX	PHONE / FAX
E-MAIL	E-MAIL

QR

NAME

ADDRESS

CITY / STATE / ZIP

PHONE / FAX

E-MAIL

The High Line Bridge at Valley City crosses the broad Sheyenne River Valley and is an imposing structure even from a distance. It was built between 1906 and 1908 by the Northern Pacific Railway as an alternative to pulling heavy trains out of the valley. The "viaduct," as it is called by the railroad, spans almost three-quarters of a mile and rises 160 feet above the riverbed. Because it was on the main line of the Northern Pacific, the bridge was guarded during both World Wars to prevent sabotage. Passenger trains continued to run through the city proper.

NAME

ADDRESS

CITY / STATE / ZIP

PHONE / FAX

E-MAIL

NAME

ADDRESS

CITY / STATE / ZIP

PHONE / FAX

E-MAIL

NAME

ADDRESS

CITY / STATE / ZIP

PHONE / FAX

E-MAIL

NAME

ADDRESS

CITY / STATE / ZIP

PHONE / FAX

E-MAIL

NAME

ADDRESS

CITY / STATE / ZIP

PHONE / FAX

E-MAIL

NAME

ADDRESS

CITY / STATE / ZIP

PHONE / FAX

E-MAIL

N P HIGH LINE FROM CHAUTAUQUA PARK
VALLEY CITY N D

VALLEY CITY

East Side, Bisbee, No. Dak.

BISBEE

Civil War veteran Col. Andrew Bisbee arrived in Towner County to take up a homestead claim in 1885. Col. Bisbee, who lost a leg at the Battle of Fair Oaks, was revered by many of his neighbors. So much so, that when the community was founded in 1888 at the junction of Great Northern and the Soo Line railroads, the citizens of the community named the town in Col. Bisbee's honor. This undated postcard shows some of the buildings on the east side of Bisbee.

S

NAME

ADDRESS

CITY / STATE / ZIP

PHONE / FAX

E-MAIL

NAME

ADDRESS

CITY / STATE / ZIP

PHONE / FAX

E-MAIL

NAME

ADDRESS

CITY / STATE / ZIP

PHONE / FAX

E-MAIL

NAME

ADDRESS

CITY / STATE / ZIP

PHONE / FAX

E-MAIL

NAME

ADDRESS

CITY / STATE / ZIP

PHONE / FAX

E-MAIL

NAME

ADDRESS

CITY / STATE / ZIP

PHONE / FAX

E-MAIL

NAME

ADDRESS

CITY / STATE / ZIP

PHONE / FAX

E-MAIL

S

NAME

ADDRESS

CITY / STATE / ZIP

PHONE / FAX

E-MAIL

NAME

ADDRESS

CITY / STATE / ZIP

PHONE / FAX

E-MAIL

NAME

ADDRESS

CITY / STATE / ZIP

PHONE / FAX

E-MAIL

NAME

ADDRESS

CITY / STATE / ZIP

PHONE / FAX

E-MAIL

NAME

ADDRESS

CITY / STATE / ZIP

PHONE / FAX

E-MAIL

NAME

ADDRESS

CITY / STATE / ZIP

PHONE / FAX

E-MAIL

NAME

ADDRESS

CITY / STATE / ZIP

PHONE / FAX

E-MAIL

NAME

ADDRESS

CITY / STATE / ZIP

PHONE / FAX

E-MAIL

S

NAME	NAME
ADDRESS	ADDRESS
CITY / STATE / ZIP	CITY / STATE / ZIP
PHONE / FAX	PHONE / FAX
E-MAIL	E-MAIL
NAME	NAME
ADDRESS	ADDRESS
CITY / STATE / ZIP	CITY / STATE / ZIP
PHONE / FAX	PHONE / FAX
E-MAIL	E-MAIL
NAME	NAME
ADDRESS	ADDRESS
CITY / STATE / ZIP	CITY / STATE / ZIP
PHONE / FAX	PHONE / FAX
E-MAIL	E-MAIL
NAME	NAME
ADDRESS	ADDRESS
CITY / STATE / ZIP	CITY / STATE / ZIP
PHONE / FAX	PHONE / FAX
E-MAIL	E-MAIL

S

Orlin C. Sarles came to Hillsboro in 1881. He was attracted by news of the area's rich farmland and saw many opportunities in the newly settled Red River Valley. He opened Valley Lumber Company with his brother Elmore Y. Sarles who served as governor of North Dakota from 1905 to 1907. He also started First National Bank of Hillsboro with his brothers, and served as the bank's vice president. These enterprises proved to be quite prosperous. O.C. was involved in the civic affairs of Hillsboro, serving for a time as mayor. He died in 1919.

O. C. Sarles, Residence 4th Ave. and Grandin St., Hillsboro, N. D.

HILLSBORO

DICKINSON

Cattle were not the only animals raised in southwestern North Dakota. Sheep also were a common sight on the range. Dickinson was perhaps the major wool-shipping point in the region in the early years. A warehouse was erected for free storage of wool in 1896 and more than a million pounds of wool were shipped out in 1900. A wool press existed by 1901 that compacted and baled the wool, which significantly reduced freight costs. This postcard image, by J.A. Osborn of Dickinson, documents wool being transported in the early 1900s to Dickinson by area ranchers and farmers from across southwest North Dakota.

T

T

NAME

ADDRESS

CITY / STATE / ZIP

PHONE / FAX

E-MAIL

NAME

ADDRESS

CITY / STATE / ZIP

PHONE / FAX

E-MAIL

NAME

ADDRESS

CITY / STATE / ZIP

PHONE / FAX

E-MAIL

NAME

ADDRESS

CITY / STATE / ZIP

PHONE / FAX

E-MAIL

NAME

ADDRESS

CITY / STATE / ZIP

PHONE / FAX

E-MAIL

NAME

ADDRESS

CITY / STATE / ZIP

PHONE / FAX

E-MAIL

NAME

ADDRESS

CITY / STATE / ZIP

PHONE / FAX

E-MAIL

NAME

ADDRESS

CITY / STATE / ZIP

PHONE / FAX

E-MAIL

T

NAME

ADDRESS

CITY / STATE / ZIP

PHONE / FAX

E-MAIL

NAME

ADDRESS

CITY / STATE / ZIP

PHONE / FAX

E-MAIL

NAME

ADDRESS

CITY / STATE / ZIP

PHONE / FAX

E-MAIL

NAME

ADDRESS

CITY / STATE / ZIP

PHONE / FAX

E-MAIL

NAME

ADDRESS

CITY / STATE / ZIP

PHONE / FAX

E-MAIL

NAME

ADDRESS

CITY / STATE / ZIP

PHONE / FAX

E-MAIL

NAME

ADDRESS

CITY / STATE / ZIP

PHONE / FAX

E-MAIL

NAME

ADDRESS

CITY / STATE / ZIP

PHONE / FAX

E-MAIL

The Marquis de Mores, a French nobleman, came to western Dakota to try his luck with the cattle bonanza. He founded the town of Medora in 1883, naming it after his wife. He was convinced the best place to slaughter beef for eastern markets was out west where the herds were. He erected a meat packing plant at Medora, but by 1886 his business ventures crashed and he returned to his native France. Medora would become famous, however, due to one of de Mores' neighbors, the future U.S. president, Theodore Roosevelt, who ranched nearby from 1883 to 1886. Roosevelt once stated, "I would not have been president had it not been for my experience in North Dakota."

NAME

ADDRESS

CITY / STATE / ZIP

PHONE / FAX

E-MAIL

NAME

ADDRESS

CITY / STATE / ZIP

PHONE / FAX

E-MAIL

NAME

ADDRESS

CITY / STATE / ZIP

PHONE / FAX

E-MAIL

NAME

ADDRESS

CITY / STATE / ZIP

PHONE / FAX

E-MAIL

NAME

ADDRESS

CITY / STATE / ZIP

PHONE / FAX

E-MAIL

NAME

ADDRESS

CITY / STATE / ZIP

PHONE / FAX

E-MAIL

NAME

ADDRESS

CITY / STATE / ZIP

PHONE / FAX

E-MAIL

Medora, Billings Co., N. D. President Roosevelt once ranched in this Valley.

MEDORA

Great Northern Depot, Grand Forks, N. D.

GRAND FORKS

Red River steamboats established the town of Grand Forks at the confluence of the Red Lake and Red rivers in 1874. The rivers were the major mode of transportation until the St. Paul, Minneapolis & Manitoba Railway, later known as the Great Northern, completed its line from Fargo in 1880. The Northern Pacific Railway also arrived in the city in 1882. The Great Northern Depot, designed by architect Cass Gilbert, opened in 1892. With the arrival of the railroad, Grand Forks quickly became the commercial center for the northern Red River Valley in North Dakota and northwest Minnesota.

U V

NAME

ADDRESS

CITY / STATE / ZIP

PHONE / FAX

E-MAIL

NAME

ADDRESS

CITY / STATE / ZIP

PHONE / FAX

E-MAIL

NAME

ADDRESS

CITY / STATE / ZIP

PHONE / FAX

E-MAIL

NAME

ADDRESS

CITY / STATE / ZIP

PHONE / FAX

E-MAIL

NAME

ADDRESS

CITY / STATE / ZIP

PHONE / FAX

E-MAIL

NAME

ADDRESS

CITY / STATE / ZIP

PHONE / FAX

E-MAIL

NAME

ADDRESS

CITY / STATE / ZIP

PHONE / FAX

E-MAIL

U
V

NAME	NAME
ADDRESS	ADDRESS
CITY / STATE / ZIP	CITY / STATE / ZIP
PHONE / FAX	PHONE / FAX
E-MAIL	E-MAIL
NAME	NAME
ADDRESS	ADDRESS
CITY / STATE / ZIP	CITY / STATE / ZIP
PHONE / FAX	PHONE / FAX
E-MAIL	E-MAIL
NAME	NAME
ADDRESS	ADDRESS
CITY / STATE / ZIP	CITY / STATE / ZIP
PHONE / FAX	PHONE / FAX
E-MAIL	E-MAIL
NAME	NAME
ADDRESS	ADDRESS
CITY / STATE / ZIP	CITY / STATE / ZIP
PHONE / FAX	PHONE / FAX
E-MAIL	E-MAIL

U V

NAME	NAME
ADDRESS	ADDRESS
CITY / STATE / ZIP	CITY / STATE / ZIP
PHONE / FAX	PHONE / FAX
E-MAIL	E-MAIL
NAME	NAME
ADDRESS	ADDRESS
CITY / STATE / ZIP	CITY / STATE / ZIP
PHONE / FAX	PHONE / FAX
E-MAIL	E-MAIL
NAME	NAME
ADDRESS	ADDRESS
CITY / STATE / ZIP	CITY / STATE / ZIP
PHONE / FAX	PHONE / FAX
E-MAIL	E-MAIL
NAME	NAME
ADDRESS	ADDRESS
CITY / STATE / ZIP	CITY / STATE / ZIP
PHONE / FAX	PHONE / FAX
E-MAIL	E-MAIL

U V

Mandan sprang up on the west bank of the Missouri River where the Northern Pacific Railway crossed "Big Muddy." A post office was established in 1878 and was called Morton, then Lincoln, before taking the name Mandan in honor of the local Indians. The name Mandan is derived from *Mantahni* or "people of the river bank." The town quickly grew becoming a major retail and railroad center for western North Dakota. Just south of Mandan is the Slant Indian Village, an early settlement of the Mandan Indians, and also Fort Abraham Lincoln, where post commander Gen. George Armstrong Custer and the 7th U.S. Cavalry left for the Little Big Horn in 1876.

Bird's Eye View of Mandan, N. D.

MANDAN

ST. MARY'S ABBEY, RICHARDTON, N. D.

RICHARDTON

St. Mary's Abbey Church is one of the architectural jewels on the North Dakota prairies. Assumption Abbey owes its existence to the tireless work of Father Vincent Wehrle who left his native Switzerland as a Benedictine monk in 1882. He was encouraged in 1899 to establish a monastery in southwestern North Dakota among the German Russian immigrant communities. He chose Richardton as the site and immediately building began. Construction began in 1905 on the monumental Bavarian Romanesque Abbey church and by 1908 was completed enough to be used. Two years later Wehrle was appointed the first bishop of the newly established Diocese of Bismarck. The Abbey still stands as a beacon for travelers along I94 and recently has gone through extensive renovation and renewal.

W X

NAME

ADDRESS

CITY / STATE / ZIP

PHONE / FAX

E-MAIL

NAME

ADDRESS

CITY / STATE / ZIP

PHONE / FAX

E-MAIL

NAME

ADDRESS

CITY / STATE / ZIP

PHONE / FAX

E-MAIL

NAME

ADDRESS

CITY / STATE / ZIP

PHONE / FAX

E-MAIL

NAME

ADDRESS

CITY / STATE / ZIP

PHONE / FAX

E-MAIL

NAME

ADDRESS

CITY / STATE / ZIP

PHONE / FAX

E-MAIL

NAME

ADDRESS

CITY / STATE / ZIP

PHONE / FAX

E-MAIL

W X

NAME	NAME
ADDRESS	ADDRESS
CITY / STATE / ZIP	CITY / STATE / ZIP
PHONE / FAX	PHONE / FAX
E-MAIL	E-MAIL
NAME	NAME
ADDRESS	ADDRESS
CITY / STATE / ZIP	CITY / STATE / ZIP
PHONE / FAX	PHONE / FAX
E-MAIL	E-MAIL
NAME	NAME
ADDRESS	ADDRESS
CITY / STATE / ZIP	CITY / STATE / ZIP
PHONE / FAX	PHONE / FAX
E-MAIL	E-MAIL
NAME	NAME
ADDRESS	ADDRESS
CITY / STATE / ZIP	CITY / STATE / ZIP
PHONE / FAX	PHONE / FAX
E-MAIL	E-MAIL

W
X

NAME	NAME
ADDRESS	ADDRESS
CITY / STATE / ZIP	CITY / STATE / ZIP
PHONE / FAX	PHONE / FAX
E-MAIL	E-MAIL
NAME	NAME
ADDRESS	ADDRESS
CITY / STATE / ZIP	CITY / STATE / ZIP
PHONE / FAX	PHONE / FAX
E-MAIL	E-MAIL
NAME	NAME
ADDRESS	ADDRESS
CITY / STATE / ZIP	CITY / STATE / ZIP
PHONE / FAX	PHONE / FAX
E-MAIL	E-MAIL
NAME	NAME
ADDRESS	ADDRESS
CITY / STATE / ZIP	CITY / STATE / ZIP
PHONE / FAX	PHONE / FAX
E-MAIL	E-MAIL

W X

A Congregational pastor who served Wibaux, Mont., and Sentinel Butte, N.D., began holding services in 1903 at the section house in Beach, a town located near the Montana-North Dakota border. Within the next few years the meetings began to grow, and the Congregational Church of Beach was organized Oct. 1, 1905. The first church building, seen here, was completed in 1909, serving as the congregation's home until 1961, when it was razed and a new, larger structure was constructed.

NAME

ADDRESS

CITY / STATE / ZIP

PHONE / FAX

E-MAIL

NAME

ADDRESS

CITY / STATE / ZIP

PHONE / FAX

E-MAIL

NAME

ADDRESS

CITY / STATE / ZIP

PHONE / FAX

E-MAIL

NAME

ADDRESS

CITY / STATE / ZIP

PHONE / FAX

E-MAIL

NAME

ADDRESS

CITY / STATE / ZIP

PHONE / FAX

E-MAIL

NAME

ADDRESS

CITY / STATE / ZIP

PHONE / FAX

E-MAIL

NAME

ADDRESS

CITY / STATE / ZIP

PHONE / FAX

E-MAIL

Congregational Church, Beach, N. D.

BEACH

Panorama View of Towner, N.D. looking South from Top of Elevator

TOWNER

Towner, along the newly laid Great Northern Railway, was officially established by the Northwest Land Company, which began selling lots in 1887. The town was named for Confederate veteran Col. Oscar M. Towner who arrived in 1884. He settled on farmland, appointed himself as McHenry County commissioner and offered his name for the new town that also was chosen as the permanent county seat. The town became a thriving regional trade center. After fire consumed the wood-frame courthouse, a new one was built, completed in 1908, and seen here as a landmark in the town.

Y
Z

NAME

ADDRESS

CITY / STATE / ZIP

PHONE / FAX

E-MAIL

NAME

ADDRESS

CITY / STATE / ZIP

PHONE / FAX

E-MAIL

NAME

ADDRESS

CITY / STATE / ZIP

PHONE / FAX

E-MAIL

NAME

ADDRESS

CITY / STATE / ZIP

PHONE / FAX

E-MAIL

NAME

ADDRESS

CITY / STATE / ZIP

PHONE / FAX

E-MAIL

NAME

ADDRESS

CITY / STATE / ZIP

PHONE / FAX

E-MAIL

NAME

ADDRESS

CITY / STATE / ZIP

PHONE / FAX

E-MAIL

Y
Z

NAME

ADDRESS

CITY / STATE / ZIP

PHONE / FAX

E-MAIL

NAME

ADDRESS

CITY / STATE / ZIP

PHONE / FAX

E-MAIL

NAME

ADDRESS

CITY / STATE / ZIP

PHONE / FAX

E-MAIL

NAME

ADDRESS

CITY / STATE / ZIP

PHONE / FAX

E-MAIL

NAME

ADDRESS

CITY / STATE / ZIP

PHONE / FAX

E-MAIL

NAME

ADDRESS

CITY / STATE / ZIP

PHONE / FAX

E-MAIL

NAME

ADDRESS

CITY / STATE / ZIP

PHONE / FAX

E-MAIL

NAME

ADDRESS

CITY / STATE / ZIP

PHONE / FAX

E-MAIL

Y Z

NAME
ADDRESS
CITY / STATE / ZIP
PHONE / FAX
E-MAIL

NAME
ADDRESS
CITY / STATE / ZIP
PHONE / FAX
E-MAIL

NAME
ADDRESS
CITY / STATE / ZIP
PHONE / FAX
E-MAIL

NAME
ADDRESS
CITY / STATE / ZIP
PHONE / FAX
E-MAIL

NAME
ADDRESS
CITY / STATE / ZIP
PHONE / FAX
E-MAIL

NAME
ADDRESS
CITY / STATE / ZIP
PHONE / FAX
E-MAIL

NAME
ADDRESS
CITY / STATE / ZIP
PHONE / FAX
E-MAIL

NAME
ADDRESS
CITY / STATE / ZIP
PHONE / FAX
E-MAIL

Y Z

NAME

ADDRESS

CITY / STATE / ZIP

PHONE / FAX

E-MAIL

Bowdon was platted by Richard Sykes in 1899 and named after his hometown in England. Situated on the Northern Pacific Railway, the town grew quickly, and within less than a year it had a population of 302. Like many newly established towns, this "end-of-the-line" town had its wild and rough elements, a place where a woman did not venture out alone at night. The houses seen here show the beginning of the town's residential district, likely around 1910.

NAME

ADDRESS

CITY / STATE / ZIP

PHONE / FAX

E-MAIL

NAME

ADDRESS

CITY / STATE / ZIP

PHONE / FAX

E-MAIL

NAME

ADDRESS

CITY / STATE / ZIP

PHONE / FAX

E-MAIL

NAME

ADDRESS

CITY / STATE / ZIP

PHONE / FAX

E-MAIL

NAME

ADDRESS

CITY / STATE / ZIP

PHONE / FAX

E-MAIL

NAME

ADDRESS

CITY / STATE / ZIP

PHONE / FAX

E-MAIL

A Residence District, Bowdon, North Dakota

BOWDON

Dakota Hall, State Normal Industrial School, Ellendale, No. Dak.

ELLENDALE

JANUARY

During the North Dakota Constitutional Convention, a provision was added to the constitution that an industrial school for manual training was to be located in Ellendale. Lack of state funding kept the school from opening until 1899 when its first building, Carnegie Hall, was completed. Teacher training began at the institution in 1907. The school became known as the University of North Dakota-Ellendale branch in 1965. A disastrous fire destroyed Carnegie Hall in 1970, and, after this event, the state closed the institution. Pictured here is Dakotah Hall, erected as a women's dormitory in 1907. Today it is the campus of Trinity Bible College.

1 _____
2 _____
3 _____
4 _____
5 _____
6 _____
7 _____
8 _____
9 _____
10 _____
11 _____
12 _____
13 _____
14 _____
15 _____
16 _____
17 _____
18 _____
19 _____
20 _____
21 _____
22 _____
23 _____
24 _____
25 _____
26 _____
27 _____
28 _____
29 _____
30 _____
31 _____

FEBRUARY

1 _____

2 _____

3 _____

4 _____

5 _____

6 _____

7 _____

8 _____

9 _____

10 _____

11 _____

12 _____

13 _____

14 _____

15 _____

16 _____

17 _____

18 _____

19 _____

20 _____

21 _____

22 _____

23 _____

24 _____

25 _____

26 _____

27 _____

28 _____

29 _____

Survey crews made their way through Bowman in fall 1905 and spring 1906 to plot the course of the new Chicago, Milwaukee, St. Paul & Pacific Railroad line. This generated much anticipation for the citizens of the community. On Nov. 16, 1907, the construction crew could be seen rounding the bend just outside of town, and by the end of the next day the first train reached the community of Bowman. A boxcar was used as the depot until a more permanent structure was built. This depot served Bowman until passenger service was discontinued in 1964.

GRAIN ELEVATORS AND R. R. STATION, BOWMAN, N. DAK.

BOWMAN

High School, Oakes, N.D.

Printed in Germany

OAKES

MARCH

Education was one of the most important issues addressed by the early settlers of a community. The school building often reflected the importance given to education. As seen in this scene in Oakes, the school likely was the most prominent structure in the town. The central building was completed in 1899 and had so much room the second floor was rented to the local Masonic Lodge. Additions were built quickly in 1903 and 1905. As early as 1891 they extended the school year to nine months and had all 12 grades, with the first high school graduates in 1892. The school was woefully inadequate by 1920 and in a public vote only five people voted against a new school. In 1924 Oakes had a new school that is still in use today.

1 _____
2 _____
3 _____
4 _____
5 _____
6 _____
7 _____
8 _____
9 _____
10 _____
11 _____
12 _____
13 _____
14 _____
15 _____
16 _____
17 _____
18 _____
19 _____
20 _____
21 _____
22 _____
23 _____
24 _____
25 _____
26 _____
27 _____
28 _____
29 _____
30 _____
31 _____

APRIL

1 _____

2 _____

3 _____

4 _____

5 _____

6 _____

7 _____

8 _____

9 _____

10 _____

11 _____

12 _____

13 _____

14 _____

15 _____

16 _____

17 _____

18 _____

19 _____

20 _____

21 _____

22 _____

23 _____

24 _____

25 _____

26 _____

27 _____

28 _____

29 _____

30 _____

The North Dakota First Legislative Assembly established the North Dakota Veterans Home in 1891. Ninety acres of land in the Sheyenne River Valley were purchased for $3,500. The Orff Brothers, a Minneapolis architectural firm, designed the first barracks building, completed Aug. 1, 1893, when the first resident, Civil War veteran George Hutchings, moved in. Serving as the barracks building until 1950, it was replaced by a larger and more up-to-date structure.

North Dakota Soldiers

LISBON

East Side of Main Street, Williston, N. D.

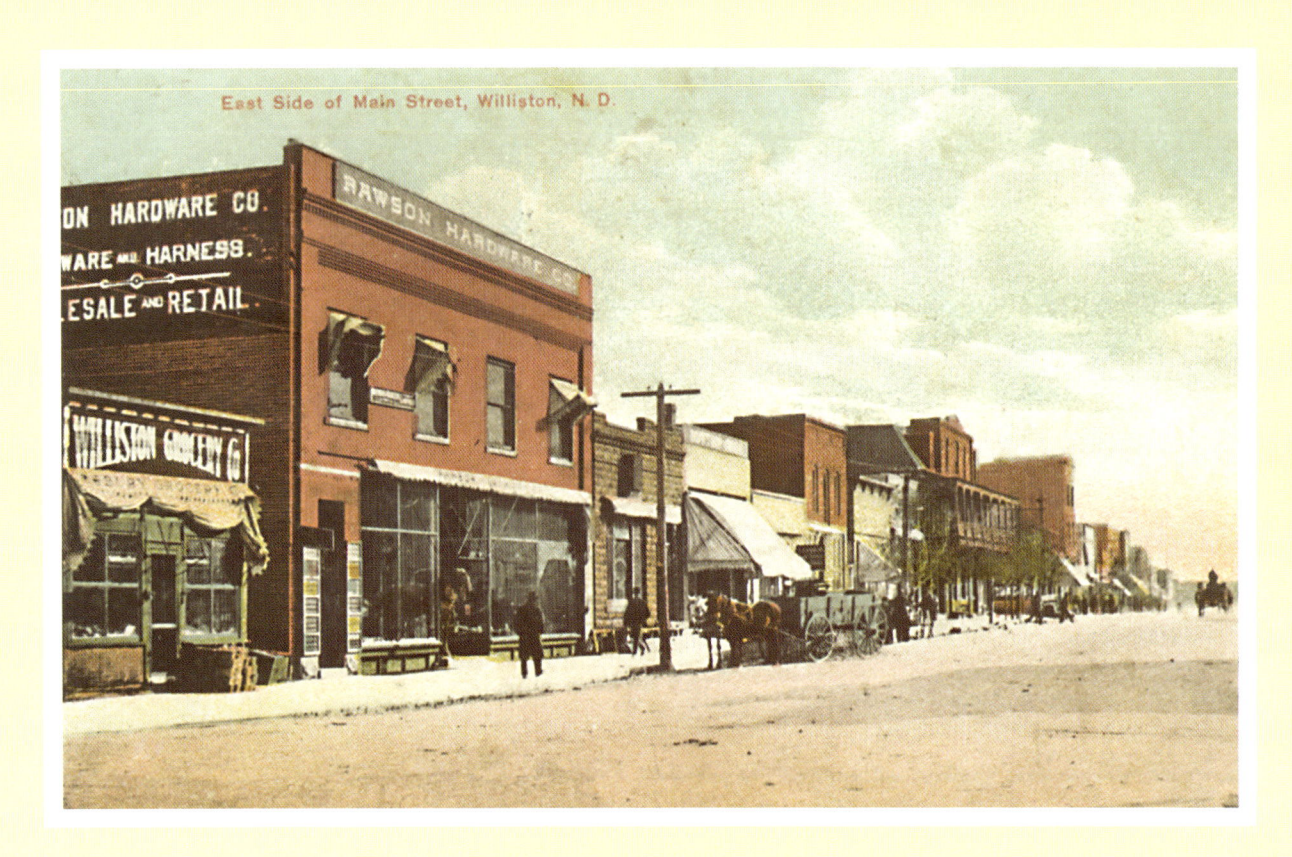

WILLISTON

MAY

As the Great Northern Railway laid tracks across western North Dakota and into eastern Montana, towns were established and people quickly followed setting up businesses and settling the prairie. The railroad arrived at the site of Williston in 1887. The city grew quickly and became the largest in the northwestern part of the state. Retail and wholesale businesses were established to serve a large rural area that was quickly growing with homesteaders and land seekers. This view shows a portion of Williston's commercial growth that took place in only 20 years.

1 _____
2 _____
3 _____
4 _____
5 _____
6 _____
7 _____
8 _____
9 _____
10 _____
11 _____
12 _____
13 _____
14 _____
15 _____
16 _____
17 _____
18 _____
19 _____
20 _____
21 _____
22 _____
23 _____
24 _____
25 _____
26 _____
27 _____
28 _____
29 _____
30 _____
31 _____

JUNE

1 ___
2 ___
3 ___
4 ___
5 ___
6 ___
7 ___
8 ___
9 ___
10 ___
11 ___
12 ___
13 ___
14 ___
15 ___
16 ___
17 ___
18 ___
19 ___
20 ___
21 ___
22 ___
23 ___
24 ___
25 ___
26 ___
27 ___
28 ___
29 ___
30 ___

James A. Pendroy was one of the first settlers to homestead on the shores of Spring Lake. When the Great Northern Railroad plotted the town site of Denbigh on his property, Pendroy became the village's first postmaster in 1900. One of the town's biggest businesses was a brick plant, which produced brick for the Denbigh school house, as well as for the school houses in Surry, Norwich and Granville. The school can be seen as the most prominent building on this postcard, postmarked in 1910.

Birdseye View, Denbigh, N. D.

DENBIGH

Main Street, Langdon, N. D.

LANGDON

JULY

Had it not been for a chance meeting of two strangers, the city of Langdon may not have been established. A hungry stranger approached Patrick McHugh in Deadwood, S.D., and asked if he would give him some food. McHugh trusted his instinct and obliged. The next day the man paid him and they parted ways. A few years later, McHugh found himself in Grafton, N.D., failing in the real estate business. By accident, the two met again, and remembering the kindness of McHugh, the man, Jud LaMoure, said he was a friend of Great Northern Railway president, James Hill. LaMoure gave McHugh a tip that the railroad was being extended north, and some fortunes could be made. McHugh and a friend with some money headed up to the area that was to become Langdon. They started the town site in 1884 and by that summer it became the county seat of Cavalier County.

1 _____

2 _____

3 _____

4 _____

5 _____

6 _____

7 _____

8 _____

9 _____

10 _____

11 _____

12 _____

13 _____

14 _____

15 _____

16 _____

17 _____

18 _____

19 _____

20 _____

21 _____

22 _____

23 _____

24 _____

25 _____

26 _____

27 _____

28 _____

29 _____

30 _____

31 _____

AUGUST

1
2
3
4
5
6
7
8
9
10
11
12
13
14
15
16
17
18
19
20
21
22
23
24
25
26
27
28
29
30
31

Joseph C. Henvis, whose homestead encompassed the town site, named it Fairmount in 1884. Henvis agreed to give up his property only if he could have naming rights. He chose the name Fairmount, after Fairmount Park located in his home city of Philadelphia, Penn. It is claimed that Fairmount was the only place in North Dakota that was serviced by four different railroads: the Fairmount & Veblen, Milwaukee Road, the Great Northern and the Soo Line. This view shows the north side of Main Street on one of its busier days.

North Side of Main St., Fairmount, N. D.

FAIRMOUNT

Soo Depot, Egeland, N. D.

EGELAND

SEPTEMBER

When the Soo Line Railroad founded the town site of Egeland in 1905, it built a depot using the company's "Standard Second-Class" design. This depot design allowed for two-bedroom living quarters on the second floor for the depot agent, directly above the waiting room and office. The building's ornamental roof brackets and second story living quarters made it easy to identify as a Soo Line structure. This type of structure was used in many of North Dakota's Soo Line depots built between 1891 and the 1920s.

1 _____
2 _____
3 _____
4 _____
5 _____
6 _____
7 _____
8 _____
9 _____
10 _____
11 _____
12 _____
13 _____
14 _____
15 _____
16 _____
17 _____
18 _____
19 _____
20 _____
21 _____
22 _____
23 _____
24 _____
25 _____
26 _____
27 _____
28 _____
29 _____
30 _____

OCTOBER

1 _____

2 _____

3 _____

4 _____

5 _____

6 _____

7 _____

8 _____

9 _____

10 _____

11 _____

12 _____

13 _____

14 _____

15 _____

16 _____

17 _____

18 _____

19 _____

20 _____

21 _____

22 _____

23 _____

24 _____

25 _____

26 _____

27 _____

28 _____

29 _____

30 _____

31 _____

Ashley, the county seat of McIntosh County, was founded in 1888. The first European settlers in the area were of Scotch and English descent; however, by the late 19th and early 20th centuries, a large influx of German Russian immigrants shaped the community's cultural identity. The German Russians of Ashley still take great pride in their heritage. Grain elevators, or the "skyscrapers" of the prairie, dominate the skyline. In 1912 there were seven elevator companies in the town.

West Side, Ashley, N. D

ASHLEY

2477 — Lincoln Hotel, Northwood, N.D.

NORTHWOOD

NOVEMBER

A devastating fire started Sept. 12, 1899, in the National Hotel building and spread through the entire business district of Northwood. P.S. Evanson built a new brick hotel in 1900 on the ruins of the National Hotel, naming it the Lincoln Hotel. The hotel was located in a prime location close to the railroad depot, making it a convenient stopping point for weary travelers. But as was the case with most small town hotels, the rise of the automobile and decline of railroad passenger service meant less patronage. Rooms in the hotel were turned into apartments, and the dining room into a dentist's office. The Lincoln Hotel closed down sometime after 1984.

1 _____

2 _____

3 _____

4 _____

5 _____

6 _____

7 _____

8 _____

9 _____

10 _____

11 _____

12 _____

13 _____

14 _____

15 _____

16 _____

17 _____

18 _____

19 _____

20 _____

21 _____

22 _____

23 _____

24 _____

25 _____

26 _____

27 _____

28 _____

29 _____

30 _____

DECEMBER

1 _____

2 _____

3 _____

4 _____

5 _____

6 _____

7 _____

8 _____

9 _____

10 _____

11 _____

12 _____

13 _____

14 _____

15 _____

16 _____

17 _____

18 _____

19 _____

20 _____

21 _____

22 _____

23 _____

24 _____

25 _____

26 _____

27 _____

28 _____

29 _____

30 _____

31 _____

Mott was founded in 1904 and the first children's education classes were held by 1907. Due to inadequate facilities, a new school was opened for grade school and high school classes in fall 1911. After several additions to the building, it is still standing. A teacher at the school mailed this postcard in 1914. She wrote: "Tho't you might like to see our H.S. at Mott. There are 10 of us here now teaching with another to be hired to assist in grammar room which is overcrowded. I like my work here very much – teach shorthand, typewriting, bookkeeping, German, also have a class in sewing. We have a good supt. – Leone"

Mott High School, Mott, N. Dak.

MOTT

ABOUT THE POSTCARDS

Two postcard collections are featured in this book — those collected and saved by Lawrence Aasen and his mother Clara Brenden Aasen, and a collection of North Dakota town postcards collected by retired Fargo physician Ronald Olin. Together they provide an amazing glimpse of the many small towns that dotted the North Dakota countryside in the early 20th century. The featured postcards date from the early 1900s to the 1930s. They represent some of the best examples produced during the "golden age" of postcards from circa 1907 to World War I. Many today could be considered works of art, particularly those printed in color.

Clara Brenden Aasen was a resident of Hillsboro, N.D. In the early 1900s she saved almost 500 postcards that she carefully preserved in a big leather album. Most of them were mailed between her and her future husband Theodore Aasen. The cards tell of flirting, parties, dances, the crops and, of course, the weather. Some of the images featured humor, romance, as well as holiday greetings. Together the postcards provide a wonderful glimpse into the lives of two young North Dakotans.

The album was handed down to their son Lawrence who continued to add to the collection, particularly more contemporary postcard scenes of his native state. Wishing to share this rich collection with others, the book *North Dakota Postcards 1900-1930* was published in 1999 featuring a sampling of the postcards his mother so carefully preserved.

A year later he wrote *North Dakota,* a book featuring many photographs taken by his parents, telling the story of a North Dakota family through good times and hard times.

Ronald Olin, native of Winnipeg, Manitoba, practiced medicine in Fargo from 1964 until retiring in 1988. One of Dr. Olin's long-time interests has been postal history. He is a charter member of the North Dakota Postal History Society and has published numerous articles on North Dakota postcards and postal history. Dr. Olin also has collected extensively postcard images of North Dakota cities and towns. He donated his postcard collection to the Institute for Regional Studies in 2005. There are more than 10,000 items in the collection and undoubtedly is the most extensive such collection found in a North Dakota archives.

Some 950 North Dakota cities and towns are represented in his collection. Not only does the collection include the diversity of cities and towns in the state, but it also includes the depth of images published for some of the larger cities. Fargo alone includes more than 1,100 postcards, Bismarck includes 400 images, and Grand Forks more than 570.

These two collections are a rich visual record documenting the settlement of North Dakota and the Northern Great Plains. They show the towns platted, the schools and churches established, and the hopes and aspirations the early settlers had in their new American frontier home.